# My Twenty First Year

## Charlotte Earl

BookLeaf Publishing

India | USA | UK

Presentation by *BookLeaf Publishing*

Web: www.bookleafpub.com

E-mail: info@bookleafpub.com

ISBN:

First edition 2022

# DEDICATION

To my family and friends,

Thank you for believing in me and supporting me, even when I didn't believe in myself. I love you all and hope to make you proud.

# ACKNOWLEDGEMENT

To all of my English teachers,
Thank you for helping me find my voice and realise my deep love for writing. I owe it all to you.

# Let's Begin with Love

I may not have told you
I love you
but those words were written
on my lips
and you knew it.

you touch me
without laying a finger
on my skin.
just the thought of you
fills me
with a welcoming ache.

# Lacking

Even when you leave
I am carrying
The weight of your absence
On my shoulders.

Drag my soul along the floor
Like an old picnic blanket.
It's okay.
You can lift it,
Pitch it up like a tent.
Use my heart strings
To keep this
Fabricated love together.

It may take some strength,
It may even feel inviting.
Just don't expect
To be welcome inside.

# Growing

honey spills
from the dimple
in your cheek.
let the amber light
soak into your skin.
the rose petals
pressed into your palm
have crushed and curled.
but you
you are glowing
growing.

# Unsaid

4

I don't want to bite down
On my tongue
For much longer.
Let the bruised words bleed out
From my mouth.

Bathing in the bitter memories
Of the past.
The sweet hope of the future.
Don't let what I think
Remain unsaid.

# Summer

sweet perfumes
sticky
in the prickling heat.

we sweat
and breathe
and live.

# Shy Girl

Don't underestimate the shy girl.
The girl who has swallowed many tongues.
Who bites down on her lip,
Swollen and purple.
Who mutters softly
Through gritted teeth.
Whose clenched fists are folded tightly
Around the silence,
Gripping onto emptiness.

Letters explode in her mind
One by one.
Itching to escape from her head,
Land in her mouth,
Roll down to the tip of her tongue,
Force their way past a broken smile.

Don't underestimate the shy girl.
For when she finds her voice and
Spits out the words,
The song will be magical.

# Wished

I wished I could have
let myself love you
because I still saw
the longing for love
in your eyes,
the pain of staring
at someone who did not
glance back.

It is heartbreaking,
I am sorry.

# Take Me Home

As fear sparked in my eyes
You kept me calm.
Saw the walking wound I was
And came to be my balm.
Held me together
When I didn't even know
I was splitting apart.
A warm hug
On the coldest of days.
Touch my skin
And take me home.
You're the best I've ever known.

# Sense of Self

You settle into your body
The way a house settles
Into the earth beneath it.
What a grounding feeling it is
To know yourself.

To really see yourself
And recognise your reflection
Staring back
Instead of expecting it
To blink.

# Stick Around

sipping on honey whiskey
under the violet sky.
hold me close
as our fingers intertwine.

stick to me
like the perfume on my neck.
your scent
is one I will never forget.

# Dear Body

Dear Body,

Thank you for being my temporary housing.
One day I will leave,
But I'll make sure to leave a good review,
And I'll tell those who knew of you
To never forget you, too.

Lots of love,

Soul.

# Let Love In

how can I think of something all the time
yet be scared of it?
maybe because I've never experienced it
fully before
never let myself feel enough
for the right people.

often put myself in the hands of the wrong ones
but I can't always blame them
because sometimes it was me
leading others towards me
when I should have shown them the door
as soon as they walked in.

I am sorry to those who claimed to love me.
I am sorry I couldn't return that love.

it was back when being sure of myself
was something I kept only to myself
because a tiny part of me had doubt
that I would not be good enough at loving
the way I was born to.

if I show my true self
to the people I desperately want to love

then what?
I'll have to keep the door open
which is difficult
and terrifying.

but I can't wait to stand by that door
and let love in.

# Advice

if you take the advice
you're giving freely to others
and hand it back to yourself,
your mind will be richer
and you will be grateful
for yourself.

# Used



will I find out who you chose
instead of me?

will you side with your selfishness and
take advantage of someone's generosity
instead of returning the love you receive?

I guess I was naive
and you knew that.

I am too far away from your heart
to know what it means for you
to really love someone
without using them.

# I Still Care

you kept me around
because you knew
I'd bend over backwards
for you.

and when you left
you knew
I'd still be here
waiting for you.

I hate that I still care.

# Eternal

don't worry
when our time is up
and our bodies say goodbye
we don't leave the earth
we become it.

# No Explanation Needed

There's no point
In trying to explain yourself
To those who don't respect you
As a human being.
To those who turn a blind eye
To your feelings.

It's like trying to see the world
From the back of your head,
Or like talking to a brick wall instead.
You won't get very far.

# Now

My back against the wall
Repeating yesterday in my head.
Why can't I just forget
And look towards today instead?

Too caught up in the past
To appreciate living for now.
It's easier said than done
I just need to know how.

So I'll begin by staring life in the face,
Tell myself to let things be.
Because in no time at all,
A memory will be all that's left of me.

# Our Story

We all want to believe
We're the heroes of our own story.
Right the wrongs of life,
Take home all the glory.

But when we're stuck
Fighting with ourselves,
Isn't it so much easier
To fight with someone else?

I've heard too many times that
Hurt people hurt people.
Can't we change the narrative
And use love as the sequel?

When we choose to rise
Instead of sinking in our lies,
Only then will we realise
That living for ourselves now
Instead of tearing others down
Is what it truly means
To be alive.

# Good Enough

I find it too easy to starve,
Forget that I need to feed myself.
I've been taught that a woman
Should stay small
In every aspect of her life.
Shrink down
So she can only see herself
In the reflection of a man's eyes.

We are taught
To satisfy men's greed
Whilst ignoring our own needs.
I'm sick of being selfless,
Strengthening the egos of men
Who constantly find ways
To tell us we are broken.

I'm hungry.
Not for the food that fills my stomach,
But for a feeling I have yet to taste.
Perhaps it's the feeling that
Women can one day be
Good enough.

# Finding Comfort

Despite us all living
Our own lives
With our own unique minds;
As humans,
We are not all that different
From one another.

We all use recycled words
To express universal emotions.
Trying to find ways
To knit sentences together,
To make them mean something.
Something bigger than us.
Desperate to help ourselves believe
In ourselves,
While proving to others
They are not alone.

We all want to live comfortably
In a complicated world.
Trying to make sense of
The feeling of being alive.